# Food To Wolf Down
## Unleashed

Dedicated to my Wife and kids.

Thank you for believing in me!

Nothing is impossible when I see your faces.

I love you x

Text Copyright © 2020 by Chef Gary Guiney

Photography Copyright © 2020 by Elaine Guiney
(Except where stated)

Wolf Logo Copyright © 2020 by Chef Gary Guiney

Copyright © 2020 by Chef Gary Guiney

All rights reserved. No part of this publication may be reproduced, transmitted, stored, etc. without the written permission of the author.

# #Unleashed

# Content

**6** Introduction

## Breakfast Section

**11** Irish Cheese and Chive Boxty, Smoked Salmon and Dill Mustard Creme Fraiche

**14** The Quick And Easy 'Good Morning Mr Wolf' Porridge Duo

**17** Green Eggs And Ham On Toasted Wheaten Bread

## Soups And Salads

**20** Beetroot, Apple And Mint Gazpacho

**23** Spiced Garlic Prawns, Cauliflower And Citrus Mixed Leaf Salad

**25** Butternut Squash, Lentil And Roasted Red Pepper Hummus Soup

**28** Greek Salad With Green pea Fusilli

**30** Indian Roasted Sweet potato Butternut Squash And Apple Soup

## Main Meals

**33** Beef And Ale Stew

**35** Little Wolfies Chicken And Chorizo Bake

**38** Pan seared Chimichurri Chicken, Multigrain Tagliatelle And Broccoli

**41** Jerk Chicken With Chilli, Mango And Pear Slaw

**44** Harissa Chicken, Pancetta And Chorizo Risotto

**47** Baked Cajun Panko Crumb Chicken Parmesan In Tomato, Basil And Garlic Sauce

## Fake-Aways

**52** Creamy Chicken Korma With Mango And Mint Lassi

**56** Korean Fried Chicken

**60** Chicken And Lamb Bhuna With Aloo Gobi

**64** Korean Beef Bulgogi And Chilli Garlic And Red Pepper Noodles

**67** Hong Kong Style Sweet And Sour Chicken

**70** Tandoori Chicken Masala

**74** Char Siu Pork, Braised Red Cabbage And Asian Greens

## The Wolf's Top 5 Dishes

**77** The Ultimate Chipotle Chilli, Smoked Bacon And Nacho Mac And Cheese

**81** Buffalo Chicken Caesar With Blue Cheese Ranch Dressing

**84** The Wolf's Elvis Sandwich

**87** Spicy Apex Chicken Stack, Champ And Pepper Sauce With Tobacco Onions

**92** Spiced Sausage Roll With Green Chilli Sauce

## Sweet Treats

**96** Skillet Pan Chocolate Brownies

**99** Blueberry, Honey And Pecan Crisp Crumble

**103** Dark Chocolate And Orange Peanut Butter Cups

## The Wolf And The Artisans

**106** Benoit/Gra Bia, Hani/Baladi Foods, Tracey/Lush Larder, Bronagh/Bakehouse, Shane & Dot/NearyNógs, Tara & Callum/Taste Joy & Declan/Erne Larder


**126** The Wolf's Final Bite

**127** Acknowledgements And Special Thanks

# **Introduction**

I told you the Wolf would be back again.

It feels like forever since I started this journey with 'Food To Wolf Down' which went on to help others in the kitchen and off course outside the kitchen. It went on to be an international seller which is something I have been so proud of. I'm so happy that you guys have been a part of that journey so thank you.

So what has been happening? Well I have always had the vision for the Food to Wolf Down Books to become a series of books. One where I can take some of my creations and share them with everyone because one thing that we can all agree on, is that food brings us all closer together, where we can share our recipes and teach our kids the vital skills that they will all need in later years. For me, this series is my legacy for my wife and children. As my father used to say "Here for a good time, not a long time". Holy Hell this just got dark and it's only the intro hahaha!

So myself, I have always had that 'Wolf Mentality' where I have always taken ownership for the path I have walked. I'm always on the attack to better, not only my own life but my family's lives and also the people around me. Yes, I can be a proud guy who feels at times he has to go it alone - like a lonewolf.

Along the way, I have met so many amazing people who have not only inspired me but I'm lucky enough to be able to call them my friends. From local artisan heroes, to little fans (wolf cubs) to foodies, influencers - they have put their faith in me and have stood by my side. They have taught me that I'm not a lone wolf anymore. I consider all these amazing people a part of the Wolf Pack.

# THE HUNT

I can remember from an early age my dad waking me and my older brother up early on the weekends. If not for Saturday morning football on Mallusk playing fields, but for us to go fishing with him and my grandad. This involved dad building a campfire for the rainbow trout we would hopefully catch, gut, clean and cook.

This gave me insight for what hunting was about - to provide food. In case we caught nothing, there was always a plan B - cooking beans, in the can, on that fire while we fished away...

There was one day which still gets talked about a lot these days, which of course we laugh about at the expense of my older brother Brian. It involved a missing boy, a pair of red wellies, my dad and grandad looking for said missing boy, while I swung upside down on a tree over a blazing fire... We were good kids… really.

So the story goes, my father was shouting out my brother's name while my grandad went up river looking for him. All of a sudden, down the river, my dad sees two little red welly boots, upside down, just floating by causally. He rushed to pull the red wellies out of the water. On the end of these welly boots was my brother Brian. He had fallen into the river but luckily my dad managed to get him in time. Thank god for bright red boots, eh!

We caught a few things that day:

1. A slap around the ear for our shenanigans
2. A few fish
3. My dad's catch of the day - my older brother.

## Artisan markets

My other memories of Guiney Weekends was with my Mum, Dad, brothers and sisters when we would often attend different markets. And one thing I will always remember about these places is, our cold hands, sometimes wrapped around a beautiful hot chocolate to keep us warm, while mum checked out different washing powders.

At these markets was my first ever experience of 'Artisans', from fresh smelling breads that filled your senses with joy, to the farmers shouting to people passing by "There you go love, freshly dug potatoes and carrots" then they would hand you a few grapes to try.

Back then I was a kid (and you know kids, they just want to see toys spinning on a table) you never took in these artisans and why they were shouting. Fast forward 35 years, I still go to as many markets with my own kids now and they get their hot chocolate to walk around with so what's changed? Well for me, my kids don't rush to pick up toys. They are going up to stalls to look at somebody who is selling their produce, they are interested in the artisan not the toys. They want to know where the food comes from, why the artisan makes it and, most importantly, can they have a taste?

I have full appreciation for artisans now that I am older. I don't, for example see a jar of jam on a stall. What I see is an amazing human being - or a couple - who are smiling and letting you personally into their lives. They are not shouting and screaming. They are having that one on one with you. So next time you get the chance, have a quick chat with them and see how passionate they are about their 'Art'. I can promise you, they do not have the support or wealth of big chain stores. Sometimes they are a single person or a family who work throughout the night to put food on their tables, or perhaps savings into their children's accounts.

Do I consider myself an artisan? No, but I am a local chef that understands local artisans and will always go above and beyond to stand by and promote them.

Do I believe that my cookbook will make a difference? Yes. Because you're reading this means maybe, just maybe, you believe what I do - that we can make a difference together.

So who's hungry??

# Time to #UNLEASH your Wolf!!

# Breakfast

## Irish Cheese and Chive Boxty, Smoked Salmon and Dill Mustard Creme Fraiche

Easy Irish dish for breakfast or brunch.

# Irish Cheese and Chive Boxty, Smoked Salmon and Dill Mustard Creme Fraiche

Serves 2-3

Time taken 30 mins

## Ingredients

- 10 potatoes (7 for mash, 3 for Grating)
- 60g cheddar cheese grated
- Small handful of chives chopped
- 250g Plain flour
- 2 Tsp of baking powder
- 3-4 Slices of smoked salmon
- 250 ml butter milk
- Small handful chopped dill
- 1/2 Lemon juiced
- 1 Tsp mustard
- 2 Eggs beaten

## Method

**Step 1**. Make your Creme Fraiche by chopping up a small handful of fresh dill And 2 tsp of Dijon mustard and juice of a 1/2 lemon.

**Step 2**. Put both the mashed and grated potatoes, chives and cheese in a bowl (make sure you drain the liquid/Starch out of the grated potato) Sprinkle over the flour, baking powder, beaten eggs and season with Salt & Pepper. Next mix until evenly combined. Add the Butter milk slowly until you have a pancake texture.

**Step 2**. Heat a little oil in a non-stick frying pan over a medium heat. Add a knob of butter. When the butter melts and bubbles, spoon a serving spoon size of the mixture into the frying pan.

**Step 3**. Cook for 2-3 minutes on each side until golden brown. Remember don't crowd the pan you could maybe get 3 pancakes in a standard sized pan.

**Step 4.** Remove from the pan and keep warm while you finish cooking the rest of the pancakes. Serve with a few slices of smoked salmon and a spoon of Dill Mustard Creme Fraiche.

You can also top with Some Crispy Bacon or a Poached or Fried Egg.

# Breakfast

## The Quick & Easy 'Good Morning Mr Wolf' Porridge Duo

Everyone knows that getting energised for the day can be challenging and sometimes several cups of coffee seems like a good idea but... well, we all know that coffee crash. But, if you have time to brew a coffee or two, then you have time to make one of these tasty meals that will set you up for the whole morning and are delicious!

...But, who says they are only for breakfast?

# The Berry Wolf Porridge

Serves 2 - 3

Time Taken 5 -7 mins

# The Berry Wolf Ingredients

- 100g Porridge oats
- 1/2 Cup Blueberries fresh
- 1/2 Cup of Mango
- Small handful Pumpkin Seeds
- 250ml Milk or Water
- Drizzle of Honey
- 1 pinch of Salt

# The Berry Wolf Method

**Step 1**: Place the oats and milk in a pan and slowly bring to the boil gently, always stirring throughout for about 5 mins to prevent sticking.

**Step 2**: Add a pinch of salt and take the pan off the heat. If it is too thick, add some water or warm milk.

**Step 3**: Serve with the blueberries, mango and honey.

# The Nutty Wolf Porridge

Serves 2 - 3

Time Taken 5 -7 mins

# The Nutty Wolf Ingredients

- 100g Porridge oats
- 1/2 Cup Drinking Chocolate
- Small handful of Crushed Hazelnuts
- 250ml Milk or Water
- 1/3 Cup sliced Strawberries
- Small handful of Crushed pretzels

# The Nutty Wolf Method

**Step 1:** Place oats and milk in a pan and add your chocolate drinking powder to the milk and oats. Bring to the boil gently and continue to stir for 5 mins.

**Step 2:** Remove from heat and if it is too thick, just add some water or warm milk.

**Step 3:** Serve with crushed hazelnuts, strawberries and crushed pretzel pieces!

# Breakfast

## Green Eggs & Ham On Toasted Wheaten Bread

This recipe was inspired by my son (wolf cub) Cody. This is one of his favourites of all-time stories from Dr Seuss' Green Eggs & Ham, so I thought I would try to bring the book alive in a quick breakfast form. But unlike the book and its use of 50 words, my recipe will contain a lot less ingredients. I hope you enjoy this is a simple one to do with your own cubs.

# Green Eggs & Ham On Wheaten Bread

Serves 1-2

Time taken 15 - 20 mins

## Ingredients

- 3 Large eggs beaten
- 30ml of single cream
- 2 tsp of butter
- 2 slices of wheaten bread toasted
- 1 tsp of cumin powder
- small handful of chopped chives
- 2 slices of bacon
- 2 tsp of honey or syrup
- 6 tbsp of olive oil (I used hickory smoked oil to compliment the bacon)

## Method

**Step 1**. In a bowl crack your eggs, and whisk until fully beaten, add your cream (set to side)

**Step 2**. In a shallow pan drizzle with some olive oil and once it comes to heat add your bacon you want to cook for about 5-7 mins turning it over until it's coming to a golden-brown colour then add your honey so the bacon takes that sweet and salty taste

**Step 3**. Have a pan on a medium/low heat and add the butter then in with your egg mixture, now this is important with a wooden spoon start from the outside and fold the eggs in making sure it's not sticking to your pan

**Step 4**. Add your chopped chives to the mix and cook eggs for 2-3 mins in total until fluffy and cooked.

**Step 5**. Place your first slice of toasted wheaten bread on the plate and layer your sweet bacon on top. Next on with your 2nd slice of wheaten then take your fluffy eggs and slide them on top of your wheaten bread and garnish with the beautiful Salsa Verde.

## Salsa Verde Ingredients

- salt and pepper to season
- 2 tbsp of capers
- 2 tsp of chopped garlic
- 50g chopped flat-leaf parsley
- 1 small handful chopped basil
- 1/2 lemon juice

## Salsa Verde Method

Add the capers, garlic, parsley and basil from the ingredient list above to a pestle & mortar and add the lemon juice. Then give it a good mix (see how it looks in my photo) To finish, add your lemon juice and it's ready to use.

# Salads & Soups

## Beetroot, Apple & Mint Gazpacho

This soup has an amazing colour and is so tasty and healthy!

# Beetroot, Apple & Mint Gazpacho

Serves 3-4

time 1 hour

## Ingredients

- 8 Cooked beetroots
- 1tsp Garlic
- 2 tbsp Red wine vinegar
- 2 tsp of Coriander
- 2 apples (Cored,& Chopped)
- 2 Sticks of Celery
- 3/4 mint leaves chopped
- 1/2 litre Chilled Veg Stock
- 1/2 Litre of (Water From Cooked Beetroot)

## Garnish

- 2 inches of Cucumber diced
- 1 Cooked Beetroot diced
- 2 tsp of Cream or creme Fraiche
- 2 apple slices diced

## Method

**Step 1**. Add your cooked beets to a 1/2 litre of cold water and add in the rest of the above ingredients and bring to a gentle boil . 10-15 mins

**Step 2**. Remove from the heat and allow to cool in fridge for min 1 hour keep the beet water (this can be made the night before)

**Step 3**. Once the Beetroot has cooled right down add all the ingredients into a blender and blitz up to a smooth consistency and add your chilled veg stock

**Step 4**. Serve in a Cold Soup Bowl and Garnish .


This is a real summer soup, best served chilled on a hot day. Beautiful vibrant colours, packed full of your daily vitamins so many great health benefits!

# **Salads & Soups**

## Spiced Garlic Prawns, Cauliflower & Citrus Mixed Leaf Salad

This is an amazing summer salad, that can be made in advance for a picnic. Its little heat paired with that citrus zing will be surely the talk of the table.

# Spiced Garlic Prawns, Cauliflower & Citrus Mixed Leaf Salad

Serves 2-3

Time taken: 15 mins

## Ingredients

- 150g prawns fresh or frozen
- 2 tsp of Garam masala
- 2 tsp smoked paprika
- 2 tsp of turmeric powder
- 2 tsp kashmiri chilli powder (mild chilli)
- 2 tsp cumin powder
- 2 tsp of garlic puree
- 2 lemons juiced
- 1 lime juiced
- 120g (1 bag) mixed leaf salad
- 5-6 cauliflower florets
- 2 red onions
- Small shaving of Parmesan cheese

## Method

**Step 1**: In a bowl add the prawns along with 1 tsp of each of the spices and the juice of 1 lemon and let them sit to take the flavour (if you can, do this the night before)

**Step 2**: Now if you have bought frozen prawns I would suggest you defrost them for 20-25 mins in some salted water (2 tsp salt) and when thaw then drain and use.

**Step 3**: Slice up your red onion and add to a roasting tin along with the cauliflower and the remainder of the spices (1 tsp). Drizzle over some olive oil. Cook in the oven at about 170c for 30 mins (the cauliflower should have a lovely yellow colour and fragrant smell). Once soft, remove from the oven and allow to cool.

**Step 4**: Now take your mixed leaves in a bowl, add the juice of your last lemon and lime, add in your marinated prawns, roasted cauliflower and give the salad a good toss.

**Step 5**: Plate up (see my picture) and top with some parmesan shavings

You can build this salad anyway you like, you could add toasted pine nuts, you could even use crumbled goats cheese or cubed paneer.

As always, this is Wolf Approved! Enjoy!

# Salads & Soups

## Butternut Squash, Lentil & Roasted Red Pepper Hummus Soup

Add hummus to soup… who would have thought?!

# Butternut Squash, Lentil & Roasted Red Pepper Hummus Soup

Serves 4

Time Taken 1 hour

## Ingredients

- 2 Onions (roughly chopped)
- 600g Butternut squash (roughly chopped)
- 2 Cups Red lentils
- 4 Heap Tbsp Of Roasted Red pepper Hummus by Hani.
- 2 tsp of Za' Atar Spice
- 3 tbsp of Olive Oil
- 1 Green pepper (roughly chopped)
- 1 Red pepper (Roughly chopped)
- 500ml of Veg stock
- 500 ml of Water.
- Cream to finish (optional)

# Method

**Step 1**. Place your roughly chopped veg in a roasting tin and add olive oil and Za' Atar spice and Roast in an oven. Cover with foil for 35-40 mins @180c once soft, remove from the oven and set to the side.

**Step 2**. Heat up your veg stock & water in a deep pan and add your cooked roasted veg and bring your soup to a gentle boil and remove from heat.

**Step 3**. With a soup ladle, transfer the soup to a blender or use a hand blender and add hummus to the mix.

**Step 4**. Only thing you have left to do is serve and enjoy with your choice of bread or croutons.

I made my croutons by simply cutting thick white bread into cubes. Place on an oven tray with a good drizzle of oil and Za 'atar spice cook until brown and crisp.

# Salads & Soups

## Greek Salad With Green Pea Fusilli

This is a beautiful Salad that can be eaten as a side dish or on its own. You can add if you want capers, or peppers or even switch out the cherry tomatoes for sun-dried tomatoes. In this dish I added a few of my own additions, sugar snap peas & mixed beans and tossed through some spinach. I also sprinkled over some black sesame seeds. Make it your own!

# Greek Salad With Green Pea Fusilli

Serves 2-3

Time taken: 20 mins

## Ingredients

- 250g Green pea Fusilli pasta
- 8 Cherry vine tomatoes, cut into wedges
- 1 Bag of spinach (washed)
- 1 cucumber, peeled, deseeded, then chopped (half moon)
- 1/2 Red onion sliced thin
- 10 mixed pitted olives
- 2 tsp dried oregano
- 100g of Feta cheese (cubed)
- 4-5 tbsp of olive oil (I used lemon infused Broighter Gold)
- 1/2 lemon juiced
- 3 tbsp red wine vinegar
- 1 small handful of chopped basil
- 1 good pinch of Sea Salt
- 1 good pinch of cracked black pepper

## Method

**Step 1**: Cook off your pasta as per packet instructions drain and rinse under cold water

**Step 2**: Make salad. In a large bowl, Add together tomatoes, cucumber, olives, and red onion and feta cheese

**Step 3**: In a small bowl, make the dressing by combining Red wine vinegar, lemon juice, and oregano and season with salt and pepper. Slowly add olive oil, whisking as you go. Drizzle dressing over salad.

**Step 4**: Last thing is to just mix your cold pasta with your beautiful Greek Salad and serve!

# Salads & Soups

## Indian Roasted Sweet Potato Butternut Squash & Apple Soup

When Fall approaches fast and the darker evenings come in, If you're like the wolf and you love simple, quick but really tasty comfort food, well look no further than this.

# Indian Roasted Sweet Potato Butternut Squash & Apple Soup

Serves: 5-6

Time taken: 1 hour 15 mins

## Ingredients

- 3 apples cored
- 1 large Butternut Squash,
- 4 large or 6 small sweet potatoes
- 1 litre/ 1000ml of Vegetable stock
- 1 white onion chopped
- 100ml pouring cream (optional)
- 2 tsp turmeric
- 2 tsp of cumin seeds or powder
- 2 tsp garlic puree
- 2 tsp of Smoked paprika
- 1 small handful of thyme
- 6 tbsp of olive oil (I used chilli infused)
- 1/2 cup of grated parmesan (for basket

## Method

**Step 1**: Peel and roughly chop all your veg, don't worry if it's not the same size as the soup will be blended.

**Step 2**: Put your veg into a ovenproof dish and add your spices and garlic puree along with your olive oil, give the veg a good mix then straight into your pre heated oven at 170c for 30-45 mins

**Step 3**: 20 mins in, carefully take the veg out, give it a little mix and back in. We want to make sure they are not burning.

**Step 4**: When the veg has softened, set to the side and get your pot on the stove.

**Step 5**: Add the roasted veg to the pan and add your vegetable stock, and thyme cook on medium-low heat for 15 mins (if the soup is too thick add some boiling water).

**Step 6**: While the soup is cooking take a non-stick pan once heated, sprinkle your parmesan cheese in a circle and cook for 2 mins until golden brown.

**Step 7**: using a spatula, lift off the cheese wheel and drape it over a tumbler/glass to mould the basket shape (see pic) When cool, break pieces of this off for garnish with the apple.

**Step 8**: Add 3 tbsp of Squash and Apple Chutney. Take a hand blender and blitz up your soup, season if you need to, finish with the cream and serve .

A good friend of mine has a local business called "The Lush Larder" where she grows her own fruits and veg and makes the most amazing chutneys and jams. She had kindly sent me some of her products to try out. I went with the indian infused squash and apple to compliment my soup and it worked so well.

So "Unleash YOUR Wolf" with this comfort soup (and don't worry if you make too much it can always be frozen)

Enjoy, The Wolf

# Main Meals

## Beef & Ale Stew

This awesome recipe serves 5 and can easily be adjusted to serve more or less.

# Beef & Ale Stew

Serves 4-5

Time taken: 1.5 - 2 hours

# Ingredients

- 4 Carrots (peeled and Sliced)
- 1kg of steak/beef pieces
- 1.5 litres of Beef Stock/bouillon
- 3 tbsp of tomato puree
- 2 tbsp of Dijon mustard
- 2 kg of peeled potatoes
- 100g plain flour
- 500ml of ale or stout (your choice pale or dark ale)
- 2 large onions (chopped)
- 2 tsp of garlic chopped)
- 2 tsp of smoked paprika
- 2 sprigs of fresh thyme

# Method

**step 1**: Heat up your pan with 3 tbsp of olive oil, add your chopped garlic, paprika and beef pieces cook on a medium/low heat for 5-6 mins to brown beef

**step 2**: Remove the beef from pan and set to side; in the same pan add your onions, carrots, mustard, and tomato puree and add in your plain flour

**step 3**: You want to cook out the flour for 5 mins making sure you're stirring throughout.

**step 4**: Add in the pan your choice of ale and beef stock, potatoes and add your beef pieces and thyme into the mix

**step 5**: Cook the stew on a medium heat for a good 1-2 hours until the beef is tender, and potatoes are breaking up

**Step 6**: To truly enjoy this meal, you should serve it with a nice piece of buttered bread. Try this out with your family.

# Main Meals

## Little Wolfie's Chicken & Chorizo Bake

Little Wolfie's Chicken & Chorizo Bake is a dish you can make with your little cubs, or if you both wish, have a go at themselves.

# Little Wolfie's Chicken & Chorizo Bake

Serves 4-5

Time taken 45 mins

## Ingredients

- 4 chicken breasts (sliced)
- 100g Chorizo (diced)
- 1 Red onion (sliced)
- 1 white onion (sliced)
- 1 bunch of Spring onion (sliced)
- 1 Red Pepper (Sliced)
- 1 Green Pepper (Sliced)
- 1 Yellow Pepper (sliced)
- 1 Cup of grated Cheddar & Mozzarella cheese

- 2 tsp Cumin powder
- 2 tsp of paprika
- 2 tsp of onion salt
- 2 tsp of garlic salt
- 2 tsp of Cayenne pepper
- 2 tsp of brown sugar
- 1 large Bag of nachos

## Method

**Step 1**: Heat up your pan with 2-3 tbsp of olive oil and add your sliced chicken cook until brown on a medium heat 8-10 mins.

**Step 2:** Add your Spices to the chicken, and 500 ml of cold water along with your chorizo.

**Step 3**: Next add your chopped veg and cook for another 2 mins, then turn off the heat.

**Step 4**: Now with an adults supervision, transfer the chicken & chorizo to a skillet or oven dish. Top with your nachos and Cheese and pop into the oven at 170c for 10 mins.

**Step 5**: Again, get an adult to remove the pan/dish from the oven and set on a cooling rack. The cheese should be melted and so gooey!

Garnish with your chopped spring onion and top with salsa and guacamole.

*Top Tip* - if you don't have the spices, you can buy the fajita mix and just add to chicken. You will get the same result.

It's amazing the time we spend making memories and teaching life skills. I hope you love my daughter's recipe!

This old wolf better watch out!

# Main Meals

## Pan Seared Chimichurri Chicken, Multi-Grain Tagliatelle & Broccoli

Chimichurri is an herb-based condiment that is a specialty of Argentina and Uruguay. It is typically served with grilled steaks, roasted beef and pork sausages but by now, you know I like to be different so I have served mine with chicken and I can tell you, It's just as amazing!

# Pan Seared Chimichurri Chicken, Multi-Grain Tagliatelle & Broccoli

Serves 4-5

Time taken: 45 mins

## Main Ingredients

- 4 Chicken breasts
- 6-8 Cherry tomatoes
- 500g Multigrain tagliatelle
- 4-5 Purple sprouting broccoli

## Chimichurri sauce Ingredients

- 1/2 cup olive oil
- 3 Tbsp red wine vinegar
- 1/2 cup of fresh parsley
- 1/2 cup fresh oregano or 2 tbsp dried
- 5 cloves garlic finely chopped
- 2 small green chilli chopped
- 1 small red chilli chopped (If you want an extra kick add a splash of chilli infused oil)
- 1 tsp of rock salt
- 1 tsp of black pepper

## Chimichurri Sauce Method

Add the sauce ingredients into a blender or chop roughly and add to a pestle & Mortar or small bowl.

Any extra can be kept and put through Mayo to make an amazing dipping sauce.

# Method

**Step 1**: remove your chicken breast and leave at room temperature for 10 mins. Season your chicken breasts with salt & pepper

**Step 2**: Before we start the chicken, have a pot of salted water on the boil for our veg. Now it's Go time!! Heat your pan or skillet pan to a medium heat with a good drizzle of olive oil and add your chicken to the pan, cook for 5 minutes then turn chicken over and cook for another 5 mins.

**Step 3:** Add a knob of butter to the pan and take some of your prepped Chimichurri dressing (save some for pasta too) and add to the chicken in the pan (see picture). Baste your chicken with the butter and cook for another 2-3 mins allowing the chicken to take on that amazing flavour.

**Step 4**: Remove the chicken from the pan and let it rest for 5 mins. During this time cook off your pasta as per packet instructions and blanch your broccoli (3-5) mins. Put cooked broccoli straight into cold water to prevent it over cooking.

**Step 5:** Now toss the cooked pasta through the chimichurri dressing along with your tomatoes and broccoli. Transfer to a bowl and top with your juicy chicken breast!

**Step 6**: Final step, take some parmesan and go nuts! If anybody tells you not too much parm, tell them you don't need that negativity 😜

# Main Meals

## Jerk Chicken With Chilli, Mango & Pear Slaw

Here is an absolute show stopper, the chicken can be marinated overnight to give it that extra flavour that any wolf would devour! For this dish, I was given a sample of Jerk marinade from Major Int (uk). It was amazing, thank you Alan.

# Jerk Chicken With Chilli, Mango & Pear Slaw

Serves: 3-4

Time Taken: 1 hour

## Jerk marinade Ingredients (3 breasts)

- 1 tsp ginger
- 1/2 cup fresh lime juice
- 3 tbsp dark soy sauce
- 2 Tbsp brown sugar
- 1 Small handful of thyme
- 2 tsp Five Spice
- 2 chillies chopped
- 2 tsp paprika
- 2 tsp Garlic powder
- 2 tsp of Onion salt

Take your chicken breasts or thighs, add into a sealed ziplock bag with all of the above and marinate from 3 to 24 hours in the fridge, it's up to you.

The longer the chicken is sitting in those amazing spices the more flavour it will take on.

## Chilli, Mango & Pear Slaw Ingredients

- 1/4 Red Cabbage
- 1/4 White Cabbage
- handful of chopped Spring onions
- 1 Mango peeled & Sliced
- 2 Pears peeled & Sliced
- 1 juice of a lime

## Method

**Step 1**: Remove the chicken from the fridge and allow it to rest and to come to room temperature. This will allow the chicken to cook evenly inside and out.

**Step 2**: Put a drizzle of oil in the pan, when it comes to the correct temperature, put your chicken breasts in. Give each breast a good 5 mins then flip over for a further 5 mins (normally after 10 mins one chicken breast would be cooked but because there is 3 we need to allow longer as the pan will be sharing the heat).

**Step 3**: Place the chicken in a preheated oven for 10 mins at 160c (you want that blackned look - see photo)

## Now for the slaw

**Step 4**: While the chicken is cooking, slice the red & white cabbage finely into a bowl. Add your chopped spring onions, mango, pear and the juice of 1 lime. Give the bowl a toss. Done

**Step 5**: Remove chicken and plate up with your slaw

Serve with Rice/Salad or just as is. You're the wolf! Make your own rules!

## #UnleashYourWolf

# Main Meals

## Harissa Chicken, Pancetta & Chorizo Risotto

Who doesn't love a tasty risotto?

# Harissa Chicken, Pancetta & Chorizo Risotto

Serves 3-4

Time taken 30 mins

## Ingredients

- 3 tsp Harissa paste
- 1 large white onion, fine diced
- 1 stick of celery, fine diced
- 1 litre of Chicken stock
- 100g Chorizo ring (cubed)
- 2 Chicken breasts (cubed)
- 50g Pancetta (cubed)
- 2 cups of Arborio rice
- 1/2 Cup of white wine
- 1/2 frozen peas
- 2/3 stalks of Asparagus halved
- 4 Tbsp of Butter
- 1 Tbsp Garlic puree
- 20g Grated Parmesan
- Few parmesan shavings to top
- 1 handful chopped parsley

## Method

**Step 1**: Heat the olive oil and butter in a large pan over a low–medium heat. Add the celery and onion and Garlic sweat for 10-12 minutes.

**Step 2**: Add the Harissa paste and a good pinch of salt and pepper, then stir.

Add the chicken, pancetta and chorizo and fry for about 10 minutes.

**Step 3**: Add the risotto rice and continue to cook for another 10 minutes.

Add the white wine and keep frying for a few minutes to cook of the wine

**Step 4:** Add a few ladlefuls of the stock and keep stirring. As the rice absorbs the liquid, add more of the stock (by the ladle) and stir. Stir regularly and gradually add the remaining stock as it is absorbed. If you've run out of stock before it's cooked, just add hot water instead. (top tip)

**Step 5**: Test the rice and remove from the heat once it's softened but still retains a little bite (al dente) You're looking for a consistency that's not too wet. Adjust the seasoning if necessary not too much as the cheese and stock contain salt.

**Step 6:** Stir in a good handful of grated Parmesan and the peas and i used asparagus in mine and serve

To serve, add a handful of chopped parsley, another sprinkle of Parmesan and a drizzle of olive oil.

# #UnleashYourWolf

# Main Meals

## Baked Cajun Panko Crumb Chicken Parmesan with Tomato, Basil & Garlic Sauce

This is one of those dishes that needs to be eaten to be believed!

# Baked Cajun Panko Crumb Chicken Parmesan with Tomato, Basil & Garlic Sauce

Serves 5-6
Time 40 mins

## Ingredients

- 4 chicken breasts
- 200g Panko Bread Crumbs (or normal fine breadcrumbs)
- 2 tbsp of Cajun spice
- 2 Cups of Plain flour
- 4 eggs beaten
- 300 ml cold milk
- 250g of grated mozzarella
- 1 Cup of Grated Parmesan

## For The Sauce

- 1 small bunch of Basil
- 3 tins of Chopped tomatoes (400g tin)
- 1 Tbsp of chopped Garlic (add another if your a garlic fan)
- 2 tsp of Dried Oregano
- 2 tsp of smoked paprika
- 1 pinch of Salt, Pepper and Sugar
- 2 Cups of Cold Water

# Method

**Step 1.** Take your Chicken Breast and carefully slice it up centre and pound flat with a rolling pin (great tip put chicken in cling film so it doesn't stick)

**Step 2.** In a bowl mix the cajun spice with the Panko bread crumbs and set to the side. Next take another bowl, add your milk to the Beaten eggs and set aside. Finally Add your 2 cups of plain flour to another bowl and set to the side.

**Step 3.** Preheat your skillet pan on a medium heat and take your flattened chicken with one hand dip one piece at a time in the flour, then into the egg mix then coat in the seasoned breadcrumbs and set on a plate (repeat process until it's all done).

**Step 4.** Drop the chicken into your pan for 3 mins each side until brown ( don't crowd the pan as it will reduce the heat of oil) once brown remove the chicken from the pan and set to the side..

**Step 5.** Take all your sauce ingredients and put into a blender and blitz up for 3 mins (if sauce is too thick add more water)

**Step 6**. Pour your Amazing sauce into the skillet pan and add your breaded chicken then pop the pan into the oven at 170c for 20 mins


**Step 7**. About 10 mins before the chicken is ready with oven gloves, remove from the oven and top the chicken with your grated Mozzarella and grated Parmesan. Put back into the oven until the cheese is bubbling (5 mins). Done.

Now this dish is #WolfApproved and can be served with Pasta, Rice or by itself with a nice salad.

Whichever way you decide to serve it, you will be amazed at the flavours in this dish.

# Fake-Aways

## Creamy Chicken Korma with Mango and Mint Lassi

Korma is a family favourite, especially for kids and the Mango and Mint Lassi is a cool refreshing drink that can go with any curry.

# Creamy Chicken Korma

Serves 4-5

Time 30 minutes

## Ingredients for curry:

- 4 chicken breasts cut into bite sized cubes
- 450g greek yogurt
- 1/2 Cup double cream
- 3 tbsp of plain flour
- 2 Tbsp white Sugar
- 2 onions diced
- 2 tbsp garlic puree
- 2 tbsp ginger puree
- 2 tsp cumin powder
- 2 tsp ground coriander
- 2 tsp turmeric
- 2 tsp garam masala
- 2 small deseeded chilli chopped
- 2 cups canned coconut milk
- 1 1/2 cup chicken stock
- 1/2 Cup of almonds

## Method for curry:

**Step 1**: Marinate the chicken in the yogurt for 1 hour covered in the fridge. While the chicken is marinating, heat up a large pan with a good glug of mustard or olive oil.

**Step 2:** Add your onions and gently fry for 5 mins. Next add your spices and chopped chilli and cook out spices for 5 more minutes. Add the plain flour and cook out for a further few minutes.

**Step 3:** Add in your chicken stock, your marinated chicken pieces and your coconut milk and bring to the boil. Once the sauce is bubbling, reduce the heat, add sugar then simmer for 15 minutes. Just before serving, add the cream and garnish with flaked almonds and serve with rice or naan.

See the next page for Lassi method.

# Mango Mint lassi

Serves 2-3

Time 5 minutes

## Ingredients:

- 2 Cups of fresh or frozen mango chopped
- 2 Cups of plain yogurt
- 1 small handful of fresh mint leaves
- 1/2 litre of cold milk
- 2 tbsp of Runny honey

## Method:

Add all the ingredients into a blender and blitz for 2 minutes on full power. Serve in a cold glass.

# Fake-Aways

## Korean Fried Chicken

Why pay loads for a takeaway when you can do it yourself at home?

# Korean Fried Chicken

Serves: 5-6

Time: 1 hour

## Sauce Ingredients

- 5 tbsp gochujang paste
- 3 tbsp honey
- 3 tbsp brown sugar
- 4 tbsp soy sauce
- 2 tbsp Chopped Garlic
- 2 tsp minced ginger
- 3 tbsp Chilli oil
- 1 Cup of water
- 2 tbsp sesame oil
- Good sprinkle of sesame seeds

## Ingredients

- 5 Chicken breasts
- 2 cups of Plain Flour
- 3 tbsp of Cornflour
- 1 tbsp of Paprika
- 1 tbsp of kashmiri chilli
- 1 tbsp of 5 Spice
- 1 tbsp of Onion Salt
- 1 tsp of baking powder
- 3 Egg Whites
- Garnish, 1 red chilli & 1 green chilli & small bunch of spring onions

# Main Method

**Step 1**: Slice your raw chicken and add to a bowl. Next crack your eggs (white of the egg only) into another bowl and add the above spices.

**Step 2:** In another bowl, add your plain flour, cornflour and baking powder, set to one side and bring your fryer to temperature.

**Step 3**: Add your raw chicken slices to the seasoned egg whites, then from there into your flour mix.

**Step 4**: Carefully drop your coated chicken into a fryer (don't overload the fryer, you want to keep oil hot) & cook for 5-7 mins until golden brown. Set to one side when cooked. Now it's time to get on with your sauce.

## Sauce Method

**Step 1**: In a wok or pan, fry off your onion, garlic and ginger in 3 Tbsp of oil (I used chilli oil). Cook for 5 mins then add the rest of the above sauce ingredients and cook for another 5 mins.

**Step 2**. Add your cooked chicken to the pan and give the pan a toss coating your chicken in that amazing red gochujang sauce and cook for another 3-5 mins and serve.

Can be served with noodles, or fried rice.

# Fake-Aways

## Chicken & Lamb Bhuna With Aloo Gobi

This dish takes a bit longer but is so worth it.

# Chicken & Lamb Bhuna With Aloo Gobi

Serves 4-5

Time taken: 1 hour 45 mins

## Curry Main:

# Ingredients

- 3 Chicken Breasts Cubed
- 400G lamb pieces Cubed
- 2 Tbsp Garlic & Ginger Paste
- 1 Red chilli, deseeded and chopped (add more if you wish)
- 2 onions diced (puree if you can)
- 1 Tsp turmeric powder
- 1 Tsp chilli powder
- 2 Tsp ground cumin
- 2 Tsp ground coriander
- 1 Tsp garam masala
- 350g of Passata or 1 can chopped tomatoes
- 2 Tsp of mild Curry Powder
- 3 Tbsp of vegetable oil or Ghee (butter)
- salt

# **Method**

**Step 1:** To an oven tray add the Chicken & Lamb with the curry powder, a drizzle of oil and 2 cups of water. Cover and add to the oven at a low heat at 160c for 30 mins.

**Step 2**: Puree the onion with 1/3 cup of cold water for the base, next heat up 3 Tbsp of oil in a non-stick pan

**Step 3**: Add the onion and 1 teaspoon salt and fry until brown and soft. (5-8 mins) Stir in garlic and ginger paste and turn the heat down to low for about 2 minutes.

**Step 4**: Add all the spices and cook over high heat for 5 minutes. Stir in chillies. Add tomato sauce or tinned tomatoes, cover and cook over low heat for 5 minutes.

**Step 5**: Take your lamb and chicken out of the oven. Don't drain the juices away as we are going to add it to the curry base. Cook on a low heat for 15 mins and let the curry base coat the meat.

# Aloo Gobi Side Dish:

## Ingredients

- 5 potatoes cooked and cubed
- 2 cups of cauliflower (cooked)
- 2 Tsp of cumin
- 1 Tsp of chilli powder (mild)
- 2 Tsp of Garam masala
- 1 Tsp of Turmeric powder
- 1 onion diced (I used red onion)
- 2 Tbsp of Garlic & Ginger paste

## Method

**Step 1**: In a non Stick-Pan add 3 Tbsp of oil, add the onions and cook for 5-8 mins until soft.

**Step 2:** Add your Garlic & Ginger and fry for 3 mins. Next add the rest of your spices and add to the pan your cooked potatoes and cooked Cauliflower.

**Step 3:** Cook for a total of 10 mins on a medium heat stirring throughout and serve with the curry and some rice and naan.

## #UnleashYourWolf

# Fake-Aways

## Korean Beef Bulgogi & Chilli Garlic & Red Pepper Noodles

Ok WolfPack, now it's time to really put your Alpha skills to the test! This dish involves a bit of prep time but let me tell you this will be worth every bite! I know you got this!

# Korean Beef Bulgogi & Chilli Garlic & Red Pepper Noodles

Serves 3-4

Time taken: 30 mins

## Ingredients for Korean Beef Marinade

- 400g Stir Fry beef strips
- 1/2 Cup Dark soy sauce
- 2 tablespoons light brown sugar
- 2 tbsp of sesame oil
- 2 tbsp Minced Garlic
- 1 tbsp of Minced Ginger
- 2 tbsp gochujang (Korean red pepper paste)
- 2 tablespoons vegetable oil,
- 2 cups of sliced Spring onions
- 2 tbsp of Sesame seeds (black, white or mixed)

Add All of the above into a mixing bowl and marinade for a few hours.

# Ingredients for Noodles

- 4 nests of thin or thick egg noodles
- 2 cups of Bean sprouts
- 4 tbsp of dark soy sauce
- 1 Red chilli sliced
- 2 Green chilli sliced
- 1 Onion sliced
- 3 tbsp of Sweet chilli Sauce
- 1 Garlic puree
- 1 Cup of spring onions
- 3 florets of broccoli
- 2 tbsp of Sesame oil

# Method

**Step 1**: Put a pan of water (1000ml) on the boil. Once you see it coming to the boil add your noodles. This will take about 3-4 mins (you want them with a bit of bite). Once done rinse, drain, set to one side.

**Step 2:** In a heated Wok/Pan, add your sesame oil (2 tbsp) and in your garlic, onions & chillies with your beansprouts and softened noodles. Finally add in your sweet chilli sauce and soy sauce, cook and toss for 2 mins.

Now for the final step - The Korean Beef!

**Step 3**: In a Wok or pan, drizzle in some olive oil. Once it comes to heat, add your marinated beef strips and cook on medium heat for 3-5 mins. Throw in your broccoli florets and 1 good glug of soy sauce. Finish with black & white sesame seeds and chopped spring onions. Serve with the noodles.

# #UnleashYourWolf

# Fake-Aways

## Hong Kong Style Sweet & Sour Chicken

Hey wolfpack, let's all face it, everyone loves that sinful treat now and again, but when you have a big family, sometimes takeout can cost a bit.

Well as I have always said, let this Wolf take you by the hand and show you how to make that sinful treat takeout at home quicker and more cost effective than any Chinese takeout near you!

Here is the wolf's version of the amazing Fake-away 'Hong Kong Sweet & Sour Chicken'

# Hong Kong Style Sweet & Sour Chicken

Serves 4-5

Time taken 30 mins

## Ingredients

- 4 Chicken breasts cubed or strips
- 2 Eggs beaten
- 110g Cornflour (save 2 tbsp of cornflour to thicken sauce)
- 1 large onion Chopped
- 1 Red pepper rough sliced
- 1 Yellow pepper roughly sliced
- 1 Green pepper
- 1 tbsp of red food colouring (optional for that really red effect)
- 100ml Tomato ketchup
- 70 ml of white vinegar
- 6 tbsp of Brown sugar
- 2 tbsp of Worcestershire sauce (optional I like it gives the sauce a bit more depth)
- 1/2 cup of pineapple juice
- 1/2 cup of chicken stock
- 2 cups of long grain rice (rinsed) will serve 4-6
- 1 litre of water

## Method

**Step 1** Rinse off your raw rice under cold water to get all the starch out of it and let it drain off, have your water coming to a boil and add your rice.

**Step 2** Once your rice has come to a boil, reduce the heat and keep stirring to make sure the rice is not sticking to the pot. Now turn the rice down, put a lid on and let it cook for 10-15 mins on low heat or until water has gone.

**Step 3** To make your sweet and sour sauce combine in a pot your tomato sauce, pineapple juice, vinegar, sugar, chicken stock, Worcestershire sauce and 2 tbsp of cornflour and cook over a low heat and set to the side.

**Step 4** Dip your chicken strips/chunks into the beaten egg wash and then remove and dip into the cornflour.

**Step 5** Fry the coated chicken for 5 mins until it has a golden-brown colour and set to side (you may want to do this in batches too much chicken will reduce the heat in pan)

**Step 6** In another pan fry off your onions and peppers for 3 to 5 mins then add your cooked chicken strips/chunks back into the pan. Pour over your beautiful Sweet & Sour Sauce with 1 tbsp of red food colouring (again optional)

Step 7 Plate up your cooked rice (I like to add a squeeze of lemon to the rice to give it that citrus flavour) and top with your Hong Kong Sweet & Sour Chicken

All in, this will take from start to finish around 30 mins and trust me when I say you won't order this dish again when you see how simple it is to make at home!

So, go on 'Unleash YOUR Flavour'! Feed the Wolf and come back leading the taste buds!

# Fake-Aways

## Tandoori Chicken Masala

This is one unbelievable restaurant style dish. The chicken can be marinated the day before to seal in that flavour, plus the addition of that red food colouring really makes it pop.

# Tandoori Chicken Masala

Serves 3-5

Time taken: 30 mins

## Tandoori Marinade

- 2 Cups of Greek Yogurt
- 1 tsp of Salt
- 1 tsp of tandoori masala powder
- 1 tsp ground ginger
- 1 tsp Smoked paprika
- 1 tsp turmeric powder
- 1 tsp Garam masala
- 1 tsp Cayenne
- 1 tsp of garlic powder
- 2 tsp red food coloring
- 1 lemon juiced

Marinate your chicken breasts, legs, or thighs for 12-24 hours covered in the fridge to take the flavour and colour.

## Indian Spiced Onions

- 1 large white onion chopped fine
- 2 tbsp of tomato ketchup
- 1 tsp of Kashmiri Chilli powder
- 1tsp of mango chutney
- 1 lemon juiced
- 1tsp salt
- 1 sprig of chopped mint

Take these ingredients and mix in a small bowl. Done.

# Masala Curry base

- 2 large onions
- 1 tsp of cumin
- 1 tsp garam masala
- 2 tsp chili powder(mild)
- 1tsp of ginger powder
- 2 tsp of garlic puree
- 1 tsp tandoori masala
- 1 tsp of turmeric
- 1tsp of coriander powder
- 1 tin 400g of tinned tomatoes
- 2 tsp of tomato puree
- 100ml of single cream
- 1/2 litre water

Food colouring added to the rice

# Method

Before we start the base, take out your chicken from the fridge and cook in the oven at about 180 for 20 minutes until the juices run clear. Cool and chop into chunks

**Step 1**: Blitz up your onions in a blender or hand blitzer add 1 cup of water to help blend

**Step 2:** Fry your onions off in a pan for 10 mins until the take a golden color but not burn

**Step 3:** Add your garlic, ginger and all the above spices and your chopped tandoori chicken (you should have a light brown color base)

**Step 4:** Add in your tinned tomatoes and cook for 20 mins on medium heat the add cream

**Step 5**: If the sauce is too thick just add some of the water.

**Step 6:** After 25 mins the dish will be ready, garnish with fresh coriander and serve with rice, naan or onion bhaji (recipe on following page)

# Easy Onion bhaji

## Ingredients

- 150g of plain flour or gram flour for (vegan)
- 1 tbsp of turmeric powder
- 1 tbsp of garam masala
- 1 tbsp of cumin powder
- 1 tbsp of smoked paprika
- 2 medium onions finely sliced
- 2 cups of cold water
- 1 cup of lemonade (optional I love that hint of lemon )

## Method

Add all ingredients in a bowl and make a batter add onions and make little onion balls. shallow fry for 3-5 mins turning done!

# Fake-Aways

## Char Siu Pork, Braised Red Cabbage & Asian Greens

My daughter Grace always asks for the same thing when we order in - Char Siu - so I thought I would treat her to my own version. She absolutely loved it and asked me to make it every time instead of ordering it.

Great praise indeed!

# Char Siu Pork, Braised Red Cabbage & Asian Greens

Serves 4-5

Time taken: 1 hour

## Char siu Pork marinade Ingredients

- Pork loin (1kg)
- 1/2 Cup of honey
- 1/2 Cup of Hoisin Sauce
- 1/4 Cup of Dark soy sauce
- 1/2 Cup of ketchup
- 1/2 Cup of Brown sugar
- 2 Tsp of chinese 5 spice
- 2 Tsp of Garlic powder
- 2 Tsp of Red food dye
- 2 Tsp of Rice vinegar
- 1 litre of Water

## Braised Red Cabbage Ingredients

- 1 Medium red cabbage
- 750 ml of water Image
- 1/4 cup of apple cider vinegar (or white vinegar)
- 1/2 cup of sugar
- 2 Tsp of 5 spice

## Method for Braised Cabbage

Put all of the ingredients in a saucepan on medium heat and cook for 1 hour. Stir every 20 mins and add more water if needed.

The cabbage should be soft but still have a slight bite. Think Al Dente.

This should be started first as it takes the longest.

## Method

**Step 1**: Pat dry the pork loin to remove any moisture. Add into a roasting tray and add all of the above ingredients. Cover with foil.

**Step 2**: Add the tray to a preheated oven at 180c and cook for 20 mins.

**Step 3**: When you get to the 20 min stage, remove the pork from the oven carefully. Take off the tin foil and baste the pork with the rich red marinade, then back into the oven for another 20 mins at a lower heat (about 160c)

**Step 4**: Remove from the oven and rest the pork loin on a wire rack or board to allow it to rest.


You can serve this with rice (75g per person), griddled pak choi (1 head) and braised cabbage, like I have in the photo.

# The Wolf's Top 5 Dishes

## The Ultimate Chipotle Chilli, Smoked Bacon and Nacho Mac & Cheese

This is a big favourite in our house and I know you're going to love it too!

# The Ultimate Chipotle Chilli, Smoked Bacon and Nacho Mac & Cheese

Serves 4-5

Time taken: 45 mins - 1 hour

## Ingredients

- 75g Plain flour
- 75g Butter
- 750ml of Milk
- 250g Grated Red Leicester cheese or Sharp Cheddar
- 3 tsp Smoked paprika
- 2 tsp of cayenne pepper
- 2 tsp of mustard
- 2 tsp of turmeric
- 3 tsp Chipotle chilli flakes
- 2 tsp chopped garlic
- 200g Bacon lardons
- 500g of grated mozzarella cheese
- 500g penne pasta or Macaroni pasta
- 1 packet of Cheese nachos (crushed)
- 1 packet of chilli nachos (crushed)

# Method

**Step 1**: Make your nacho cheese sauce by melting your butter in a non-stick pan, add your flour and cook for 5-10 mins low heat to cook off flour

**Step 2**: Add 2 tsp of smoked paprika, cayenne and mustard to the pan to make a Roux

**Step 3**: Have your milk heat and gradually add in the milk to the roux to your form a white sauce, next in with your turmeric to give the sauce the base of colour, keep stirring throughout process and add in your Red Leicester cheese it will take about 15 mins in total (you should have a lovely yellow colour cheese sauce)

**Step 4**: Cook your pasta off in boiling salted water as per cooking instructions and drain

**Step 5**: In a pan fry off your bacon with the garlic and the last of the smoked paprika add in your chipotle chili and cook for 5 mins, then put your cooked pasta in the pan along with all your nacho cheese sauce and give it a good mix.

**Step 6**: Add everything to an ovenproof dish or a skillet and top with the mozzarella cheese pop into a preheated oven and bake for 1 hour at 170c.

**Step 7**: Remove from the oven about 5 mins before it's ready with oven gloves because it's going to be *hot* and top with your crushed nachos. Pop back into the oven to gently toast your crisp topping.

Plate, serve and enjoy!

# #UnleashYourWolf

# The Wolf's Top 5 Dishes

## Buffalo Chicken Ceasar With Blue Cheese Ranch Dressing

This salad is in my top 5 because it pushes the boundaries of the norm and makes it your own.

# Buffalo Chicken Ceasar with blue cheese ranch dressing

Serves 2-3
Time 10 minutes

## Ingredients:

- 2 -3 chicken breasts, cooked and shredded
- 1 Baby gem lettuce
- 1 Cup Franks Hot sauce
- 1/2 small baguette sliced & toasted
- 1 Cup of Blue cheese crumbled
- 2 cups mayo
- 2 cups finely grated parmesan
- (keep 1 Cup for toasting)
- 1 Cup of Fine breadcrumbs
- 2 tbsp. lemon juice
- 6-7 Cherry Tomatoes cut
- 5-6 slices of cooked bacon cut
- 2 tsp. Worcestershire sauce
- 2 tsp. dijon mustard
- 1 tsp garlic powder
- Pinch of salt and pepper

## Method:

**Step 1**: In a small bowl, whisk together mayonnaise, parmesan cheese, lemon juice, Worcestershire sauce, mustard, salt, pepper, and garlic powder and crumbled blue cheese and set to the side

**Step 2:** Chop lettuce at the bottom and break off single leaves.

**Step 3:** In a small bowl, toss shredded chicken with buffalo sauce and leave in fridge 30 mins

to take on the flavour and colour and roughly chop your cooked bacon.

**Step 4** (Build it up): On a plate place your lettuce leaves, add a few of your cut cherry tomatoes then some of your marinated shredded buffalo chicken. Add some bacon and a spoon full of your ranch dressing.

**Step 5**: In a heated pan, add 1 cup of breadcrumbs, 1 cup of grated parmesan and toss in the pan for 3-4 mins until brown.

**Step 6**: Last thing to do is a good sprinkle of your toasted parmesan crumbs and finish with toasted croutons.

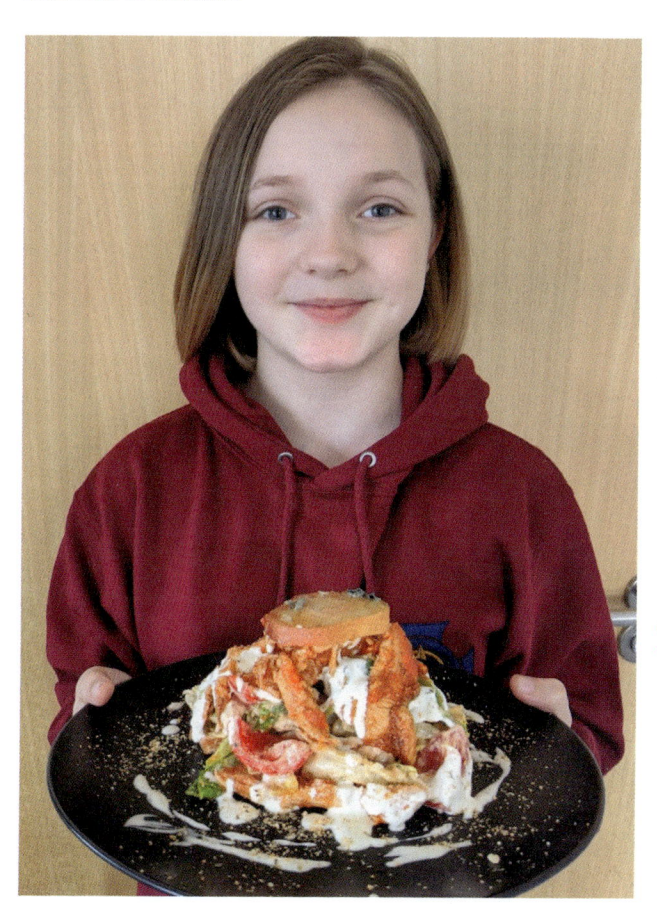

Here is the finished salad as modeled by my amazing Little Wolfie, Grace. I do hope you try her Chicken & Chorizo Bake on page 35, it is amazing!

# #UNLEASHED

# The Wolf's Top 5 Dishes

## The Wolf's Elvis Sandwich

This sandwich made my top 5 simply because of how the saltiness works with the sweet jam (and because, it's Elvis!! I mean c'mon it's King approved!) but it doesn't end there! We also add Mr Heat to the mix with the amazing spicy peanut sauce. I took a classic sandwich and just took it to another level.

# The Wolf's Elvis Sandwich

Serves 1

Time 15 minutes

## Ingredients:

- 3 slices Thick white bread
- 6 slices streaky bacon
- 700g of Smooth Peanut Butter
- 1/2 Cup of Choice of Jam (I used Blackcurrant and Chilli jam by Lush Larder)
- 1/3 Cup Dark Soy Sauce
- 2 tsp ginger powder
- 1 Heap tbsp of turmeric powder
- 1/3 cup of Sesame oil
- 2 tsp of chilli flakes
- 1/3 Cup of Sweet chilli sauce
- 1/3 Cup sriracha sauce
- 2 banana Sliced
- 3 tbsp of butter
- 500 ml warm water (add more if its too thick)

## Method:

**Step 1**: Start by Making the Spicy peanut Sauce! Put the peanut butter in a microwave bowl and heat for 60-90 secs until peanut butter has melted.

**Step 2**: Remove from the microwave and add your soy sauce, Sesame oil, sriracha, ginger powder, turmeric powder, sweet chilli sauce and chilli flakes, get a whisk and start to mix, Just add your warm water slowly while you mix. You want to have a sauce that slowly falls off the spoon. Then set sauce to the side.

**Step 3**: Place your streaky bacon on a flat oven tray and cook at 180c for 10-15 mins until crisp. While the bacon is in the oven, pop 3 slices of bread in the toaster and toast until light brown.

**Step 4**: Now to build the sandwich up! Take one slice of toasted bread, spread on some jam, put a layer of sliced banana, 2 slices of cooked bacon and a good drizzle of the peanut sauce. Add another slice of bread on top and repeat, then top with lid .

**Step 5**: In a hot pan melt the butter and put your 3 layered sandwich in the pan for 2 mins on each side until the top and bottom have a golden brown and crunchy finish. Serve!

#UNLEASHED

# The Wolf's Top 5 Dishes

## Spicy Apex Chicken Stack, Champ And Pepper Sauce With Tobacco Onions

This amazing dish will have your guests begging for more!

# Spicy Apex Chicken stack, Champ and pepper sauce with tobacco onions

Serves 5

Time 30 mins

## Ingredients for champ

- 1.5kg of Potatoes peeled and quartered
- 1 bunch of chives
- 1 cup of grated smoked cheese
- 3 heap Tbsp of butter
- 250 ml of cream
- 1 tsp of nutmeg (optional)
- Salt & Pepper to taste

## Ingredients For Apex Stack

- 2 Cups plain flour
- 2 tsp oregano
- 2 tsp smoked paprika
- 2 tsp onion salt
- 2 tsp garlic salt
- 5 chicken breasts sliced goujon style
- 200g fine breadcrumbs or panko crumbs
- 180g of Chilli heatwave doritos or cheese
- 3 large eggs
- 2 tsp of smoked paprika

## Ingredients for easy pepper sauce

- 120 ml beef stock
- 1 tbsp Worcestershire sauce
- 1 tbsp Dijon mustard
- 150ml of double cream
- 2 tsp of cracked black pepper
- Tobacco onions for garnish
- 1 large onion sliced fine
- 1 cup of plain flour
- 2 tsp oregano
- 120 ml of milk

# Method:

**Step 1:** Bring your potatoes to the boil and drain off the water. Return to heat for 2 mins to dry out excess water.

**Step 2:** You can mash these now or leave until the last step.

**Step 3**: Set up 3 mixing bowls:

<u>Bowl 1</u>: plain flour and all your herbs and spices (see photo)

<u>Bowl 2</u>: breadcrumbs, doritos, 2 tsp of paprika (see photo)

<u>Bowl 3:</u> 3 large eggs whisked

**Step 4**. With one hand take the sliced chicken and put it into the flour mix, then into the egg mix, then into your crumb mix, (see picture) then onto a tray, repeat the process until they are all coated.

**Step 5:** Heat up your deep fat fryer and add the goujons making sure you are not overloading the fryer as it will reduce the heat. Cook for 3 mins until they start to brown then place onto an oven tray and cook for 10-15 mins at 175c until cooked through (see picture).

**Step 6**: Take your sliced onions, add them to the milk. Remove them and put them into the flour then into the fryer for 1-2 mins until they float. Remove onto a tray and season with oregano and allow to dry.

**Step 7**: Pour your beef stock into a sauce pan, add the cracked black pepper, the dijon mustard and the worcestershire sauce. Then bring to heat and finish with cream.

**Step 8:** Add your cream, butter, nutmeg, cheese and chopped chive to a saucepan and bring to heat. **<u>Do not boil</u>**! Mash your potatoes and add this cream mixture. Use a spatula to fold for a creamy texture. Top with your cooked chicken, pour over your pepper sauce and finish with crispy onions!

# #unleashed

# The Wolf's Top 5 Dishes

## Spiced Sausage Roll With Green Chilli Sauce

This sausage roll is a favourite in our house and I know it will be in yours too.

# Spiced Sausage Roll With Green chilli Sauce

serves 5-6

total time 60 mins

## Ingredients:

- 500g Shop bought puff Pastry
- 3 eggs beaten
- 1 cup of flour (for rolling pastry)
- 1 tsp of turmeric (add in egg wash for colour)
- 800g Sausage meat
- 2 cups of fine breadcrumbs
- 2 tsp Cumin powder
- 2 tsp of Garam masala
- 2 onions very finely diced
- 2 tsp Garlic powder
- 1 tsp of ginger
- 2 tsp of paprika
- 2 tsp Kasmir Chilli powder
- 2 tsp of coriander

## Method:

**Step 1**: Take your sausage meat and add to a large mixing bowl. Add all your spices (except the turmeric) and breadcrumbs. Hold back on the turmeric as you are adding that to the egg wash mix.

**Step 2**: Give the sausage meat and spices a really good mix and set to side.

**Step 3**: With clean hands take your plain flour and dust your workspace, take your puff pastry and roll out the pastry in a large rectangle. Spoon the sausage mixture along the centre of the pastry. Roll up pastry with the shortest side up to the middle and then fold the longer side over the top to enclose filling. Trim off any excess pastry and make sure your sausage roll is sealed. Egg wash will do this.

**Step 4:** Now you have two options here:

**1**. you can place the sausage roll log into the oven, cook and cut into desired size. The benefits for this, is it will save shrinkage, OR:

**2**. Cut the log into the desired size and then pop into the oven to cook.

Before you do that take your egg wash and brush over your sausage roll and top with chilli flakes, poppy seeds or sesame seeds, or just leave plain, it's up to you.

**Step 5:** Place the sausage roll onto some grease proof paper and place into a preheated oven at 180c for 35-40 mins until the pastry is golden brown and cooked throughout.

## Green chilli & Mint Dipping sauce ingredients:

- 1 bunch of coriander leaves
- 1 bunch of mint leaves
- 2 small green chilli peppers
- 1 tsp of cumin powder
- 2 tsp of garlic puree
- 1 tsp of garam masala
- 1/2 cup of olive oil
- good pinch of salt
- if too thick, add water

## Method:

Deseed the green chillies and place all the ingredients into a blender then blitz until smooth, 2-3 mins.

These sausage rolls can be enjoyed on their own or had as part of a main meal with some chorizo cheese fries. These are easy to make: On top of your cooked fries/chips, put some diced chorizo, sliced red onion and grated cheese. Done!

# Sweet Treats

# Skillet Pan Chocolate Brownies

These are so easy to make and are delicious. A real sweet, chewy treat for everyone.

# Skillet Pan Chocolate Brownies

Serves 8

Time 45 minutes

## Ingredients:

- 1/2 cup unsalted butter (melted)
- 1 cup white sugar
- 1/4 cup cocoa powder
- 1 tsp vanilla extract
- 1/4 teaspoon salt
- 3 large eggs
- 1 1/2 cups plain flour
- 2 cups chocolate chips

## Method:

**Step 1**: Preheat the oven to 170c Grease your skillet pan with butter.

**Step 2**: In a large bowl, whisk together the melted butter, sugar, cocoa powder, vanilla and salt.

**Step 3**: Add the eggs one at a time, whisking each time as you add one

**Step 4**: Fold in the flour and chocolate chips just until the flour is combined. Sieved flour works better for folding.

**Step 5**: Transfer the batter into the greased skillet, smoothing it into an even layer. Sprinkle additional chocolate chips on top. (see picture above)

**Step 6**: Bake for 30 to 35 mins at 170c until the center is just set.

Remove the skillet from the oven, top the brownie with ice cream and serve immediately.

# #unleashed

# Sweet Treats

## Blueberry, Honey and Pecan Crisp Crumble

This is a delicious homemade crumble that will keep everyone happy.

# Blueberry, Honey and Pecan Crisp Crumble

Serves 8

Time 40 minutes

## Ingredients for the filling:

- 5-6 cups fresh blueberries or frozen
- 3 cups caster sugar
- 2 tbsp of lemon juice

## Ingredients for the crisp topping:

- 2 Cups of Crunchy nut cornflakes
- 1 Cup of Crunchy Granola
- 1 Cup of oats
- 1 Cup brown sugar
- 150g plain flour
- 150g chilled butter cubed
- 1 tsp of cinnamon powder
- 2 tbsp of Honey (for garnish)
- 3-4 mint leaves (optional)

## Method:

**Step 1:** preheat the oven to 180c and lightly grease your pan or oven dish

**Step 2:** Add the Blueberries, Caster sugar, lemon juice to the pan or oven dish

**Step 3:** Then on top of your blueberries, add your chopped pecans, granola mix, the crunchy nut cornflakes (see picture)

**Step 4:** In a separate bowl add your plain flour, the butter, cinnamon powder and brown sugar and work through with fingers.

**Step 5**: Finish the dish with your crumble mix and drizzle with the honey (see picture) pop the pan or oven dish into your preheated oven and bake for 30-35 mins until the blueberries are bubbling and the top is golden brown.

Serve warm with your favourite ice-cream or just get stuck in with a spoon straight from the skillet!

# #UNLEASHED

# Sweet Treats

## Dark Choc & Orange Peanut Butter Cups

Seriously morish and delicious cups, you won't want to share!

# Dark Choc & Orange Peanut Butter Cups

Serves 6-7 (4 inch tart cases) or 10-12 in Cupcake cases

Time 15 mins to prepare, 1-2 hours to set

## Ingredients:

- 150g Double chocolate digestive biscuits
- 190g Natural Smooth Peanut butter
- 1 Cup of icing Sugar
- 250g Dark cooking chocolate (melted)

## Method:

**Step 1.** Put the Chocolate biscuits into a blender and blitz until smooth, Don't worry if you don't have a blender you can put into a clear sandwich bag and smash with a rolling pin.

**Step 2.** In a bowl add the crushed biscuits, the icing sugar and peanut butter and mix until the icing sugar has blended into the mix, then form 2 inch wide discs (see photo)

**Step 3**. Take your cases if they are not cases where the bottom pops out, then put a layer of greaseproof so the mix does not stick. Pour a layer of melted chocolate to cover the base.

**Step 4**. Add one of your discs into the centre of the case (see photo) and cover with more melted chocolate.

**Step 5**. Put into the Refrigerator and chill them for 1-2 hours until set. Serve and enjoy!!

For my cups I used a local artisan Taste Joy company all natural peanut butter, but you can use any natural peanut butter.

Have fun play around with toppings, this is a really quick, simple and fun treat to do with the kids.

# The Wolf & The Artisans

To get a better understanding of our local artisans, I decided to hit the road and go on the hunt throughout N.Ireland to spend some time with a few of these local legends.

Sadly, with the covid restrictions, I did not get the chance to interview more, but I have made promises that I will hit the road again when it is safe to do so. There are so many more local artisans throughout Ireland that have stories to tell and so many more that I want to meet.

# GRÁ BIA

## Chutneys

What makes a man from Brittany decide to settle in Bryansford? The love of the countryside, the people and the food. And it is his love for cooking and creating delicious chutneys that lead Benoit Le Houérou to create Grá Bia.

Benoit first moved to Northern Ireland in 2013 having studied for a City & Guilds Diploma in Food Preparation & Cooking in a hotel in the Channel Islands.

He has always loved to cook and in his spare time he enjoyed nothing better than creating chutneys which he gave as gifts to his family and friends. Being part of the gardening team at Montalto Estate, as well as looking after his young daughter, Benoit had his hands full but he began to wonder whether his home made chutneys could be sold commercially. In 2018, he saw an advertisement for the Go For It programme and decided to apply to explore setting up a business.

In May 2019 Grá Bia Artisan Fine Foods was launched. The name Grá Bia comes from Benoit's passion for food with a 'Celtic' twist. 'Grá' means 'Love', 'Bia' means 'Food' and, as he says, "Producing delicious chutneys is all about sharing Love and Passion for Fine Foods".

We met up for a coffee in his backyard and what a beautiful backyard it was, the Tollymore Forest. So, coffees in hand - and a hot chocolate for Cody - Myself, Elaine, Cody and Benoit had a nice chat and walked through this scene of beauty.

It did not take long. Just listening to Benoit showed his love for what he does and why he does it. He is such a down to earth, humble man, that has a vision of where he wants to take his company. He works around the clock alone to produce some of the most amazing chutneys I have ever tasted.

I just know that the name Grá Bia will grow from strength to strength and I want to personally thank him for his time and wish him all the very best going forward.

Grá Bia chutneys combine fresh fruits, vegetables and spices to create wonderful flavours. There are currently 5 products in the range Beetroot & Mint; Mango & Green Chilli; Pineapple, Cranberry & Black Pepper; Rhubarb, Date & Ginger; and Tomato & Black Onion Seeds.

# *Where can you find Grá Bia Products?*

Grá Bia chutneys are on sale at a number of outlets across Northern Ireland and keep growing stockists. To find a stockist close to you visit:

# www.gra-bia.co.uk

Photograph used with permission from Benoit Le Houérou

# Baladi Foods - *The Wolf meets the King*

## Hummus

So, my first ever meeting of Hani was at an artisan market in Crumlin, Co Antrim. We had decided to go as I was going up to meet up with Tracy of Lush Larder (who you will find out more about later on). Walking around the market, I noticed a man in a red cap which read 'make hummus great again'. I had a good chuckle with my mum and wife and said I have got to go talk to this guy.

So, myself and Hani got chatting about what he does. He said to me "you won't ever taste hummus like this". Now the chef in me thought "well that's a big claim to state" as I'd say my own hummus that I make at home is pretty good. I love hummus but my wife, Elaine, LOVES hummus. We grabbed our crackers on display and tried out Hani's range. Now do you ever have that moment where you go, "woah, hold on a second"? Well, the smile on my face said it all and the look on Elaine's will probably stay with Hani forever! I will say it the claim he made about no other hummus tasting like this was no word of a lie. The freshness and the creamy texture was unlike anything I had tasted before. The flavours were out of this world.

So we swapped details that day and a friendship was born. A short while later, Hani invited Elaine and I up to his house where we also got to meet his amazing wife Sandra, who, I have to say, put on a sample of some beautiful natural spices and olive oil from Palestine for us to try. It was a first for Elaine and I and we both loved it, so thank you Sandra.

So as the four of us sat around the table chatting, it was at this point I found out so much more about Hummus by Hani & Baladi Foods.

His recipe for his hummus is an authentic recipe from Jerusalem, passed down through Hani's family. Handmade by his mother and now made by himself. He chatted a little more about his mother and he reached out to grab a book carefully placed inside protective plastic.

As he looked at this book, you could tell from his face, the love and pride of what he held in his hands. It was his mothers own handwritten recipe book. Hani states that he knows that with every tub of hummus he makes, his mother is standing beside him, guiding his hand and he lives for taking that recipe of hers and making her proud, which I know he does everyday.

### What is Baladi Foods?

Baladi Foods produces premium quality, all natural, handmade Middle Eastern foods using carefully selected ingredients.

Hani Muhtadi, founder and owner, is from Jerusalem and proudly serves his community as a food artisan. He takes pride in his craft and is passionate about producing foods that reflect the traditions and expertise of the generations before him. His food is a story of culture and nature, combining to form authentic traditional family recipes.

Hani sources the freshest, finest-quality local ingredients available to him to make decadent, flavourful and creamy hummus that is completely free from additives and preservatives. 'Hummus by Hani' contains the highest percentage of chickpeas because his recipe wasn't originally developed to sell, it was made as a delicious reminder of home. It is an authentic recipe from Jerusalem, made to feed and nourish growing families.

## Where can I find Hummus by hani?

Well, one of the main stockists of Hummus by Hani, is Indie Fude, which is situated in Comber, Newtownards or Carnbrooke Meats in Lisburn. You will also find his products at local artisan markets throughout N.Ireland. But the best way for you to order some of the best ever hummus I have ever tried, is on social media. Just look up Baladi foods. He is not hard to find and will answer any queries you may have.

# The Lush Larder

## Jams and Chutneys

I met Tracey, owner of the company 'the lush larder' on social media. She had reached out to me one day to ask if she could have my opinion on some of her range by gifting me some of her products. I had seen some of her range already and the wolf was licking his chops at the sound of some of those flavours.

*One of my dishes made using Lush Larder products*

Tracey launched The Lush Larder in October 2019. She makes small batches of artisan Jams & Chutneys in her home using local, seasonal fruits & vegetables. She also grows some of the produce herself & what she doesn't grow she would source from local farm shops.

One thing I noticed about Tracey was her ethos to support locals as much as she could, which in turn reduces food miles and carbon footprint. Being from Co Armagh, "The Orchard County", she loves to celebrate & use her local PGI Status Bramley Apple in many of her products.

From "Plot to Pot" is very much her mantra. Only the freshest produce is used for her Jams & Chutneys and the proof is in the flavour of her products. Working with seasonal produce means her flavours change with the seasons. So each season a new flavour is born.

After a lot of back and forths and striking up a great friendship with Tracey, we met up on a few occasions just for a chat and to, of course, sample some of her amazing range.

One thing that really impressed me about what she does, is the fact that lush larder is a one woman operation. She is a mother of three kids, but still has time to produce some of the most amazing jams and chutneys that N.Ireland has to offer. I can speak from experience as I have used her products in a few of my creations with my own personal spin on things.

Since 2019 The lush larder has grown as a company and so many more exciting things lie ahead for Tracey. As her work ethic is unreal, it is easy for me to be biased. I would be in contact with Tracey a lot and when she has new flavours or creations she would always share with me. I guess that is part of friendship.

## *Where can you find The Lush Larder?*

You can find The Lush Larder on social media pages like facebook and instagram tracey also currently sells her products on eBay. You can also find her products at local artisan markets, and one more bit of exciting news: she will have thelushlarder.com up and running soon.

# Bakehouse

Photograph used with permission from Bronagh Duffin

What can I tell you about the amazing Bronagh Duffin of Bakehouse? Well, my journey took me up to the home and cookery school of Bronagh, just outside Magherafelt in the village of Bellaghy. A little fact: this is the burial place of the famous Irish poet Seamus Heaney.

As soon as I pulled up in my car, I was greeted by Buster, her four legged friend, who at first was barking. 30 seconds later, he was coming up to me looking his head rubbed. Such a cute little guy.

I sat down with Bronagh and had a lovely cup of coffee and we got chatting in the amazing kitchen in which she runs her cookery classes.

For as long as she can remember, her life has always been about food. She believes strong memories are associated with food which is so important to her. Food has the power to nourish the body and mind and take us to a place of contentment and happiness with family and friends or as an individual pick me up.

One of her favourite memories is of being a child, eating her Grannies freshly baked soda bread, dripping in butter and feeling so happy and safe at that time. When life gets tough, Bronagh just cooks and bakes to take her right back to the love and homeliness of her Granny's kitchen.

She had decided to take a career break from nursing in 2017 and create Bakehouse, an "at-home" cookery school based in her own family kitchen. Her desire was to bring the gift of cooking simple, gorgeous food using local ingredients and traditional recipes to her visitors. Bronagh offers cooking, baking, demonstrations and foraging classes for all ages, in the form of private one to one sessions or for larger groups who want to spend a few fun hours learning a new skill together.

In Bronagh's eyes, cooking is not just about the final result, but the process of deciding what to cook, selecting gorgeous local ingredients, creating the layers of flavours in the dish and punctuating it with gorgeous herbs and spices to uplift the recipe.

In her cookery school she takes each visitor on a taste journey, giving them a few hours out of their busy lives to be immersed in new tastes and simple cooking techniques. Bronagh's recipes are all simple, delicious and can easily be replicated at home. "I want each one of them to feel at home in my kitchen, just as I did in my Granny's kitchen" she says.

Cooking has always been a never-ending journey for her, constantly learning about new ingredients, skills, recipes and meeting some amazingly inspiring people along the way.

The time I spent with Bronagh was just full of energy. I was actually chatting to someone who I could personally relate to, someone who has that pure love of food, who lives and breathes for what she does and this wasn't the Sloe Gin sample talking for me, haha!

Yes, I said *Sloe Gin,* made by Bronagh herself. She had offered me a sample and I just have to say, I was hooked and kindly showed me her recipe for it. I had such an amazing day and felt so welcomed. It's not everyday you invite a wolf into your home, so thank you Bronagh!

## Where to find and book Bakehouse?

Bronagh offers Gift Vouchers, Cooking classes, Beautiful Artisan afternoon tea boxes, filled full of her own bakes and products from local artisans. Check out her website at **www.bakehouseni.com** or find her on Facebook and instagram @bakehouseni

# NearyNógs Stone Ground Chocolate
## Chocolate

The last leg of my artisan journey took me and my little co-pilot, Cody, to Northern Ireland's first bean-to-bar chocolate makers and also one of the oldest in Ireland. NearyNógs chocolate is crafted in a small factory on the Mourne Coast. Their family friendly chocolate factory has breathtaking views of the Irish Sea, Carlingford Lough & the Mourne Mountains.

NearyNógs is a family business, established in 2011, originally as a fund-raiser for their eldest daughter travelling to India to do charitable work with orphans. Chocolate became a passion and a resource. Shortly after, a younger daughter became life threateningly ill and needed urgent medical treatment in Great Ormond Street Hospital London. This resulted in the formation of the family business to provide income and flexibility. The Neary family works as a team alongside a small community of friends and family, working together to make the dream a reality.

I have met both Shane and Dot Neary at some artisan markets in the past but Shane and I go years back. We met as extras in the Game of Thrones television series where we struck up our friendship, walking up hills together, swords and shields equipped. I have to say, we looked badass. I'm sure Shane would agree.

We were invited to their factory and their amazing world of chocolate, to understand and see the process of how their artisan chocolate is made. This husband and wife duo are a perfect match as they, along with their family, are the cogs that make their dream a reality. They have family and friends individually hand-sorting each cacao bean to ensure there is no dirt, twigs or stones that would ruin their amazing products.

They ethically source sustainable cacao beans, supporting the rainforest alliance and they practise direct trade where possible. They pay above market value for cacao beans, to ensure that the Cocoa farmers get a living wage, ensuring the survival of the cacao industry and the farmers livelihoods. This is to honour the farmers, the cacao and the maker. Recently, NearyNógs has switched to Solar energy, powering the chocolate factory! They are passionate about reducing carbon emissions and looking after the environment. All of their packaging is either made from recycled materials that can be recycled or is biodegradable.

The name "NearyNógs" comes from children stories written by Johnnie Neary, Shane's Dad. Stories that have never been published but the memory remains. Neary is the family name and Nógs comes from the Irish Gaelic word Tír na nÓg, which means the land of the youth or the Eternal land. Call in for a visit, see how chocolate is made from the cacao bean to bar and hear some chocolate stories.

## *Where to Find NearyNógs Stone Ground Chocolate?*

For the list of stockists, check out their website **www.nearynogs.com**

Now as I was saying previously, there were some more local artisans I had arranged to go to visit but due to this crazy pandemic, I had to unfortunately postpone to a later date. So I would love to give these artisans a special mention, as in the past I have used their products and have had many a conversation with them.

# Taste Joy Company

## Peanut Butter

Ok, hands up who is a peanut butter monster! I've stopped typing there to put both my hands up, but you are probably wondering why peanut butter? Sure, you can get this everywhere, why is peanut butter special? Well sit back, and let the wolf tell you why the Taste Joy company sets the bar high. Is it because of the numerous Irish food awards they have won? Or is it because their story is a love story? I will let you decide...

Taste Joy was established from one man's romantic gesture to win a woman's heart, so begins the story...

Taste Joy Company is a husband and wife team that started at the end of their first date back in june 2016 when Callum surprised Tara with a jar of peanut butter because she had said it made any day perfect.
Tara had always been a lover of peanut butter and Callum had found a way to win Tara's heart. So he started out on his mission to work on recipes with the hope of creating a better version of her favourite peanut butter. On christmas of 2016, he carefully wrapped up his peanut butter creations and gave them to Tara. Based on her expression and her reaction, it was obvious that refills would be required. Callum, from that day forward, made a promise to make these peanut butters for the rest of Tara's life. He proposed 3 months after knowing each Tara and saying "YES" was the easiest and quickest decision she had ever made!

As time went on, friends and family began showing interest and started placing orders and over time, the word along with their peanut butter, started to spread and then Taste Joy was born.

Their peanut butters have won many awards and I'm sure they will win many more.

Excuse the pun 'In a nutshell' Taste Joy is made with love for love, always was and always will be. It was too good to keep the lid on.

I myself have used their amazing natural and packed full of flavour peanut butters in some of my creations and stand by what I'm saying - that I fully get behind Taste Joy and I can highly recommend them. If you have not had a chance to experience that love-in-a-jar, I urge you to try them out. You will not be disappointed. All their products are palm oil free, naturally gluten free and vegan friendly.

# Where to Find Taste Joy?

Like all our artisans, you can find the amazing range on Facebook, instagram and at local artisan markets but the best way to reach out to Tara and Callum, is through their website www.tastejoyco.com

# Erne larder

## Jams, chutneys & sauces

My final Artisan comes from the same background as myself. Declan O'Donoghue is a fully trained chef who has paid his dues from the age of 16. Working in kitchens where standards are always set high to deliver the best service possible. These exceptional standards have followed him throughout the years and in October 2016, Erne Larder was born. They are a family run preserve business based in Enniskillen, Co.Fermanagh. These standards are something they pride themselves on.

They offer small batch handmade jams, chutneys & sauces made to a professional chef standard. I have used Declans products and from one chef to another, I fully understand how he is a perfectionist and nothing less will do.

His range of chutneys, jams and sauces have blown me away on so many levels because he has taken his chefs creative flair and ran with it. I have been lucky enough to try the range and anybody that knows me knows I'm honest - sometimes too honest - but I really loved the flavours that my palette experienced. I can see why his range has won the great taste awards.

I am excited about meeting up soon with Declan to grab a coffee and talk about what's next for Erne Larder. I just know whatever is next, it's going to be a huge success!

## Where to Find Erne larder?

You can find these fantastic products at local artisan markets, or reach out to Erne Larder on facebook, twitter and of course, instagram. To find the complete list of stockists and to find out more about why Declan and Erne Larder are the perfect choice for any kitchen, check out their website:

www.ernelarder.com

# The Wolf's Final Bite

This is the part of the book where I bring my story to a conclusion. When 'Unleashed' started out, it was my way of sharing my life, my recipes and my adventures with you. I won't lie, the road getting here has not been easy, with at least a few setbacks, but like the wolf, each time something got in my way I stood firm, stood true and never backed down. But this was not just *my* journey, this was my amazing wife and kids journeys too and I would not have started out on this journey without them by my side.

My aim was to take book one - Food To Wolf Down - to help you find the confidence to get back into the kitchen, for you to teach others and to help out with a charity close to my heart. I can happily say that mission was a success. With book two, this was now to take that new or re-found confidence and love you have for food and take you into that world of being creative and putting a smile on someone's face.

It was also my way of showing off what this country has to offer with our local artisans, showing you why we need more than ever to support them and how you can help them. Now with this mission, I would love to be able to say it's a huge success too, but it's an ongoing fight and I'm hoping that when the wolf looks to his side he sees you standing next to him, backing them. Together we can make a difference.

Well, as the wolf walks back into the woods, know that he will always be ready for the next hunt. Who knows what his next mission will be or where it will take him. Just know that when that day comes, if you hear a growl or a howl, know that the wolf is on the move.

#UNLEASHYOURWOLF

# The wolf's acknowledgments

The first person I want to say thank you to is the original chef/cook, one person who everyday of my life has been there for me and stood by me. Supported me even when at times I probably didn't deserve it. I have had the honour of cooking for this amazing person, she is as honest as honest can be. One time I made a soup for her and her response was "Gary, the soup was lovely but you cut the carrots too small" haha! You have to laugh. She, along with my late dad, has had such an impact in my life, from buying me knives when I was learning to being a Chef. Or lending an ear when I had a bad day at catering college.

This woman I can call a true hero, an inspiration and about a million other amazing names. She is all those things. And I am extremely lucky to be able to call her *'Mum'*.

Which brings me onto my family, my amazing and very talented wife and best friend Elaine, who has stood by me for all these years, who believed in me when a lot of people did not. I may have created and made the dishes but she made them come alive through photography.

To my amazing kids {wolf cubs} who have made me laugh time and time again, who inspire me everyday and when I look in on them at night sleeping, I know they are the reason I do what I do. For the fun we have in the kitchen together cooking, watching them grow and making dishes with me. I would never change this for the world. We are so proud of each of them. We love you.

Thank you to my brother and sisters and their other halves. I'm sorry I have made you guys drool at times, in fairness you did get to taste the famous mac & cheese of mine! Thank you for your support. It means so much to me and I love you guys.

To my best friend Mark who I have had the pleasure of cooking for and teaching some of my dishes to! C'mon mate, I don't want to see any more cans of that curry shit in your cupboards! Thanks bud, for listening to me give off when I'm pissed off!

# Special Thanks

To my friend and peer who was the first person to support me when book 1 came out. Still to this day she continues to do so. June d'Arville, thank you so much for your kindness. It blows me away and the respect I have for you and what you do, inspires me so much.

Eddie Johnson and his company Rebel vino, thank you my friend from New York City, for giving the wolf not only a place in your heart but supporting me with your advice. For pushing me even though I did not make it easy for you! We will get those cold beers one day. Best of luck with the Rebel Vino platform launch, it's going to be massive with you at the helm.

To Hama Davidson, thank you so much for supporting me but also being a huge advocate for supporting local. Thank you for the stellar advice that you have given me. But thank you mostly for being a friend who has got behind the wolf. Check her out on social media @Indianblondee

A few others I would love to give a shoutout to: Rosemary Matthews at kids kitchen cookery school, this lady is absolutely amazing and leading the way teaching the next generation of little cooks/chefs. Find her at:

www.kidskitchencookeryschool.co.uk

To Cornel and Dawn, owners of lazercraftz, who put my wolf logo onto one of their amazing chopping boards. Check out their website at:

www.lazercraftz.com

To my Number One Fan in the USA, little Chef Eli! Thank you my little friend for reaching out to me. I hope one day to see you rocking up and taking care of the artisans, state side, with your love and passion for artisans and off course great food! Keep at it kiddo!

There are so many many people I would love to say thank you to. To all my friends on social media, you know who you are. Those who have reached out to me, taken my advice and also given me advice. And last but certainly not least, **YOU**, the reader. I really hope you enjoy this book and hope it has inspired you in some way. You are all amazing in the wolf's eyes. Each and every one of us has that ability to unleash their wolf, you just need to believe it's inside you...

As this wolf heads off into the sunset, rest assured, he is not far from finished…

Much love,

Gary x

Printed in Great Britain
by Amazon